Volume 7
Decodable
Reader

Mc
Graw
Hill
Education

Bothell, WA • Chicago, IL • Columbus, OH • New York, NY

Contents

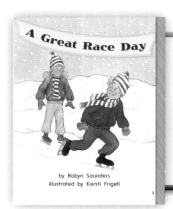

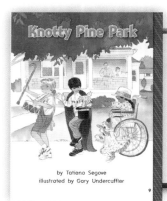

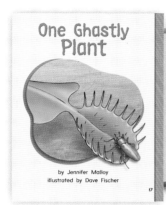
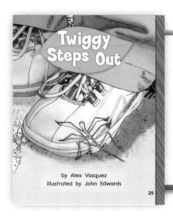

A Great Race Day

by Robyn Saunders
illustrated by Kersti Frigell

It was time for Sprat Creek's skating contest. Trey and Ava planned to skate.

"I hope I win again," Trey said.

"Hey, I think you will!" said Ava. "You are eight years old now."

They waited in line with their neighbors. This year, Trey chose to skate in the long race. Ava chose to skate in the short race. They agreed to obey the safety rules.

Trey and Ava went down to the creek.

"I see the start line," said Trey.

"Great!" said Ava. "I hope we both win prizes this year."

4

Trey thought about last year. He got first prize then. He had been the best in the short race. But this year he was in the long race. Would he still win?

"I hope I do well," said Ava.

"I think you'll win the short race!"
Trey told her as he tied his skates.

"And I think you will win the long
race!" Ava replied.

It was time for the skaters to
line up.

"This is going to be a great
race!" Trey said. "I'll see you
at the finish line!"

It had been a great race day! Both
Trey and Ava won first prize! They
hung their ribbons on their beds.

Knotty Pine Park

by Tatiana Segove

illustrated by Gary Undercuffler

Wren and her pals met at Knotty Pine Park.

"It's fun to swing and climb," said Wren. "But let's do something new."

"Let's make a parade!" said Knox.

"Yes!" cried Wren. "We can dress up."

"I'll wear my Dad's funny hat," Sasha said. "Mom got it for him but it's the wrong size."

"That's great," said Wren. "Our parade will be lots of fun!"

Wren wrapped an old sheet around her. She knotted it on the side. She got a drum and a cane. Then, she marched to Knox's house.

Knox wore a shiny black cape. He pulled a paper bird from his top hat.

"You really have a knack for tricks!" said Wren.

"Mom helped me use scissors to make this bird," Knox said.

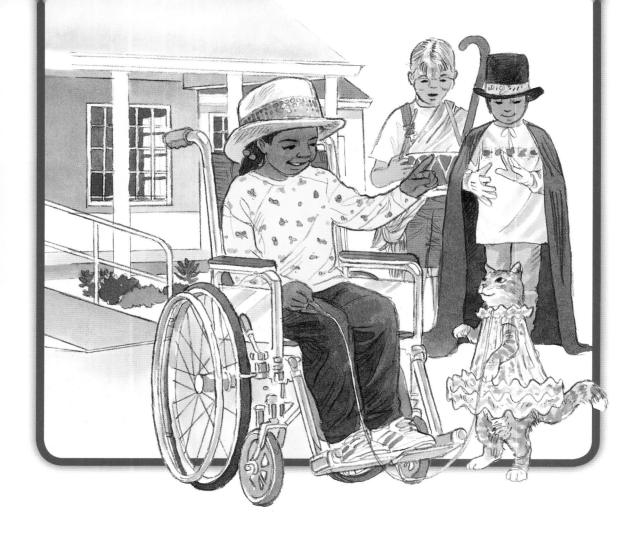

Sasha wore her dad's funny hat.
"This is my cat, Lamb," Sasha said.
"I designed this dress for her!"

"Your cat knows lots of tricks,"
said Knox.

14

Wren, Knox, and Sasha marched
down the street. Lamb danced in her
fancy dress. The three kids and Lamb
made quite a scene! People watched
the parade from their windows.

At last, Wren, Knox, and Sasha
reached the park. Kids stopped
swinging. Kids stopped climbing. They
clapped and cheered. The Knotty Pine
Park Parade was a big hit!

One Ghastly Plant

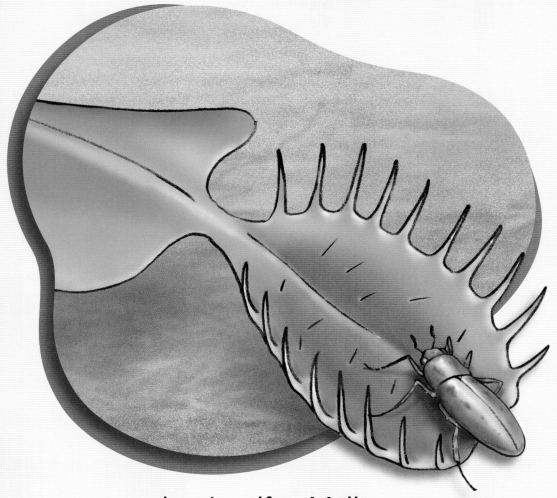

by Jennifer Malloy

illustrated by Dave Fischer

A Venus flytrap is a strange plant. Many folks think that it is a creepy plant, too. Let's see if they are right.

The Venus flytrap lives in wet places like marshes.

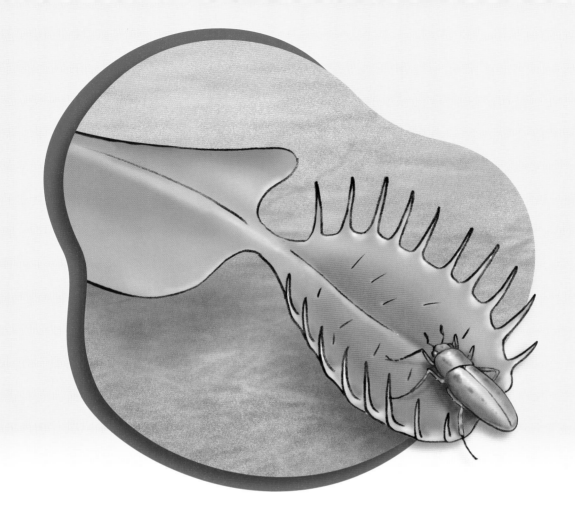

Plants need to eat. But the Venus flytrap can't get food from soil. And it can't walk to find what it needs.

It has learned to adapt, or change, to stay alive. How? The Venus flytrap catches and eats bugs!

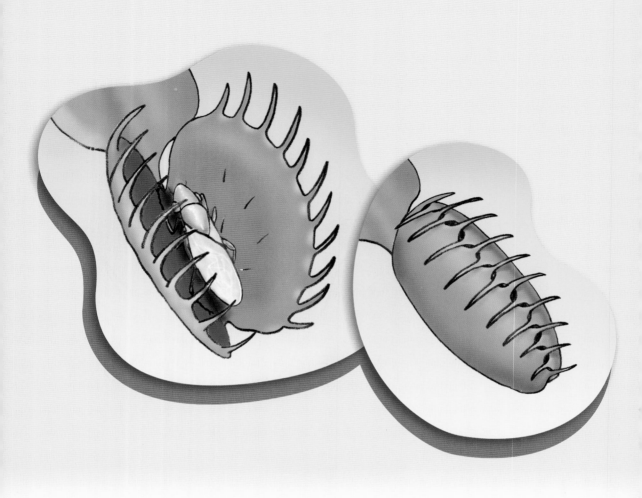

This plant has leaves that form a trap.
Inside is sticky, sweet stuff. It makes
bugs want to go in to eat it. When a
bug gets in the trap, the leaves snap
shut! The bug can't get out!

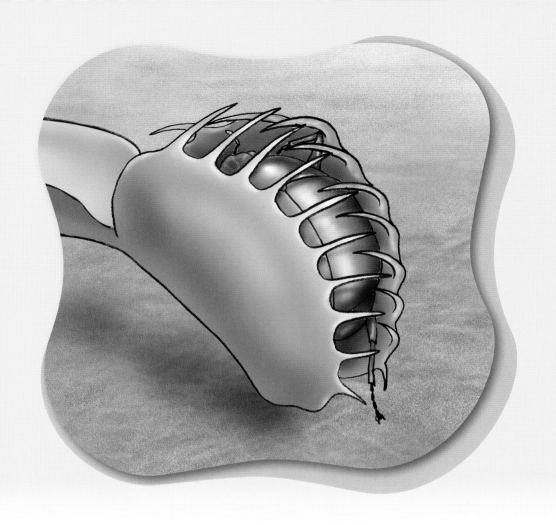

Seeing a Venus flytrap catch a bug
is a ghastly sight! This plant knows
the right size bug to catch. When
the leaves close, the plant makes an
airtight trap. This is a reliable way
to get food!

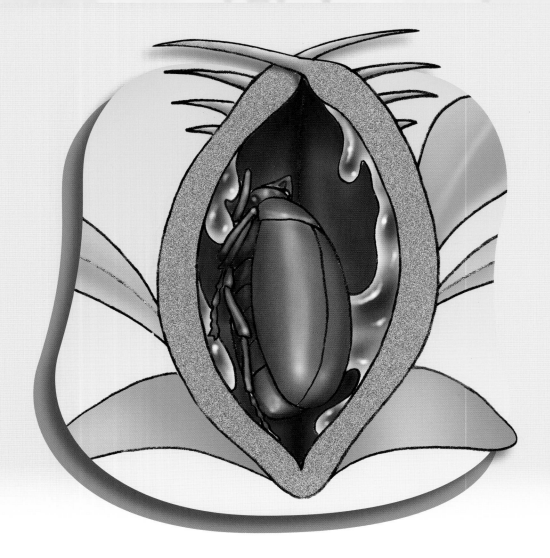

Now the bug is the plant's lunch!
Sticky acid glistens as it coats the
bug. Ugh!

The bug's freshness makes it a
really yummy treat!

Venus flytraps often grow in the wild.
But they can be in danger when
land is cleared. Now it is not legal
to dig up these plants.

You can get a Venus flytrap at a plant store. Fill a glass jar to the halfway mark with soil. Keep the plant damp and feed it with tasty bugs. This is one ghastly plant that is creepy and fun!

Twiggy Steps Out

by Alex Vasquez

illustrated by John Edwards

Some plants, like a Venus flytrap, act like an animal. But this animal looks like a plant. It is a stick insect.

We will call this one Twiggy. One day, Twiggy came out of his house. He wanted to take a look around.

Stick insects can be green or brown.
Being brown helps the insect blend in
with the ground.

Twiggy thought he found a rock. He
climbed up. He looked around.

Twiggy climbed to the top of the rock. There he found a round brown thing. Twiggy decided it was a tree. Stick insects like to eat leaves. So Twiggy climbed up to get some leaves.

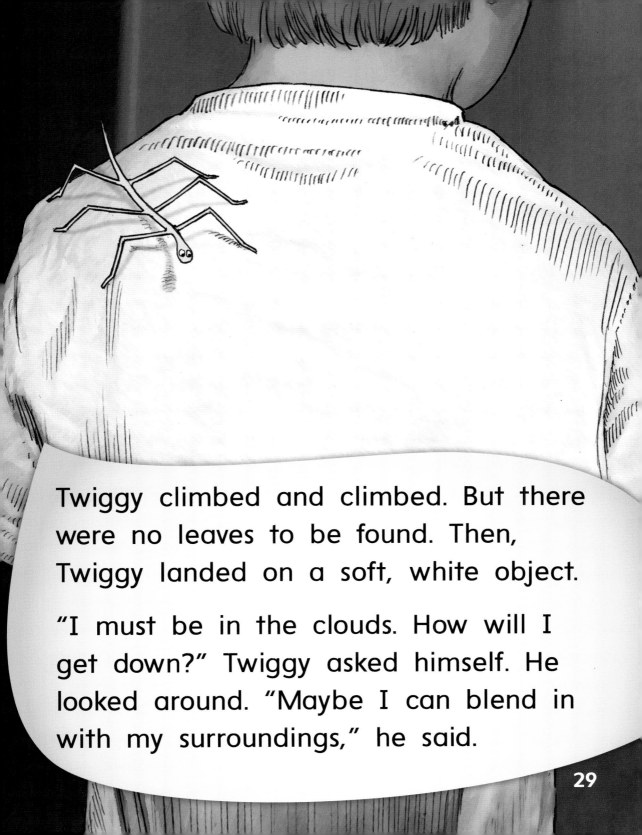

Twiggy climbed and climbed. But there were no leaves to be found. Then, Twiggy landed on a soft, white object.

"I must be in the clouds. How will I get down?" Twiggy asked himself. He looked around. "Maybe I can blend in with my surroundings," he said.

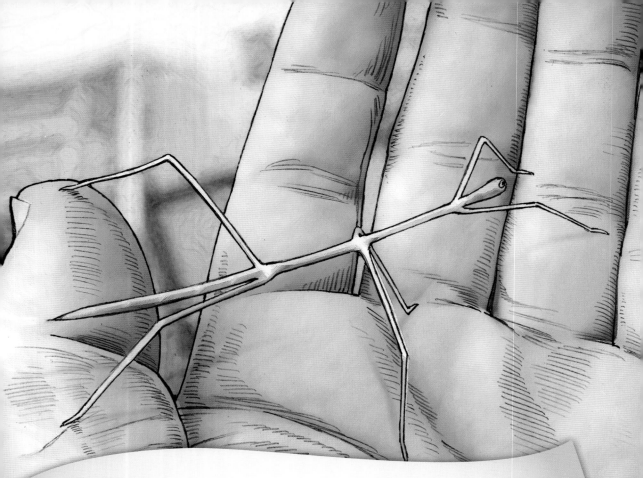

Stick insects can change color. This helps them to blend with their surroundings. But Twiggy could not turn white like this cloud. So he jumped down.

"I found a bridge!" Twiggy gasped. But the bridge suddenly ended.

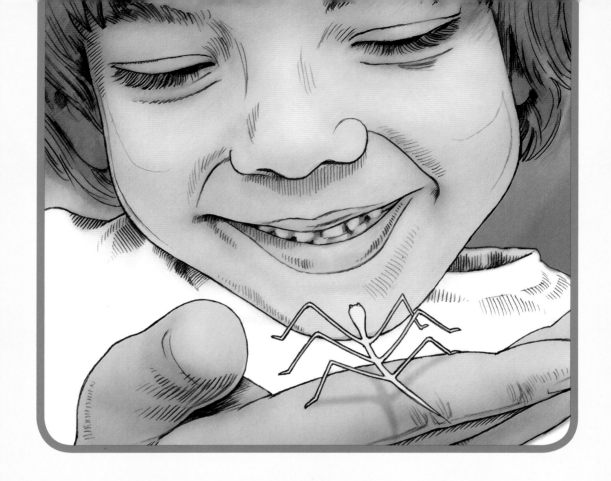

The bridge began to sway.

"No! No!" Twiggy shouted.

The bridge was rising up. Twiggy began to panic. "Why did I ever come out of my house to prowl?"

Just then the bridge gently dropped to the ground. Twiggy took a quick look around. He found his way back to his house.

The next time you see a twig on the ground, it may be a stick insect like Twiggy just out looking around!

Roy and Mr. Boy

by Chrissie Blake

illustrated by Jan Pyk

Roy was a pig. He lived on a big farm.
He enjoyed eating a lot. He enjoyed rolling
in the mud even more.

There was one thing Roy did not enjoy. That was Mr. Boy, the cat. Mr. Boy howled and howled. That annoyed Roy and spoiled his day.

"Mr. Boy annoys us all," said Ms. Joy the cow.

Troy the dog said, "He makes too much noise. We need to teach him a lesson."

Roy called a meeting of the animals.

"You can help me with my plan,"
said Roy. "We will join forces to teach
Mr. Boy to make good choices."

In the morning, Floyd the rooster
woke the animals. Mr. Boy was still
asleep. All the animals started
howling. Mr. Boy was annoyed.

Mr. Boy yelled, "Stop the noise!"
"I get the point!"

And he really did. Mr. Boy never
annoyed Roy again.

Volume 7

Decodable Words

Target Phonics Elements: Long *a: a, ea, ei, ey*
Ava, eight, great, hey, neighbor, obey, Trey

High-Frequency Words

Review: *again, about, been, down, said, their, to, was, would, you*

Story Words
thought

Decodable Words

Target Phonics Element: Silent Letters: *wr, kn, gn, mb, sc*
climbing, designed, knack, knotty, knotted, Knox, lamb, scene, scissors, wrapped, Wren, wrong

High-Frequency Words

Review: *around, do, down, new, of, our, said, something, was, your*

Story Words
parade

Decodable Words

Target Phonics Elements: Silent Letters: *gh, lf, lk, st*
*airtight, folks, ghastly, glistens, halfway, right,
sight, ugh*

High-Frequency Words

Review: *how, now, one, out, to, too, walk, what*

Story Words
food, learned, soil

Decodable Words

Target Phonics Elements: Diphthong: *ou, ow*
*around, brown, clouds, down, found, ground, how,
prowl, round, shouted, surroundings*

High-Frequency Words
Review: *come, looked(s), one, of, their, to, was, you*

Story Words
animal, color, thought, took

Word Count: 150

Decodable Words

Target Phonics Element: Diphthong: *oi, oy*
annoyed, annoys, boy, choices, enjoy, enjoyed, Floyd, join, Joy, point, Roy, spoiled, Troy

High-Frequency Words

Review: *again, all, called, lived, of, one, said, to, too, was, you*

Story Words

animals, rooster

Decoding skills taught to date:

Phonics: Phonics: Short *a*; Short *i*; Short *o*; Short *e*, Short *u*; *l*- Blends; *r*- Blends; *s* -Blends; End Blends; Long *a: a_e;* Long *i: i_e;* Long *o: o_e;* Long *u: u_e;* Soft *c*, Soft *g* ,*-dge;* Consonant Digraphs: *th, sh, -ng;* Consonant Digraphs: *ch, -tch, wh, ph;* Three-Letter Blends; Long *a: ai, ay;* Long *i: i, igh, ie, y;* Long *o: o, ow, oa, oe;* Long *e: e_e, ee, ea, e, ie;* Long *e: y, ey;* Long *u: u_e, ew, u, ue, /ûr/: er, ir, ur, or; /är/ ar; /ôr/or, oar, ore; /îr/ eer, ere, ear;/âr/ are, air, ear, ere;* Long *a: a, ea, ei, ey;* Silent Letters: *wr, kn, gn, mb, sc;* Silent Letters: *rh, gh, bt, mn, lf, lk, st;* Diphthongs: *ou, ow;* Diphthongs: *oi, oy*

Structural Analysis: Plural Nouns *-s;* Inflectional Ending *-s;* Plural Nouns *-es;* Inflectional Ending *-es;* Closed Syllables; Inflectional Ending *-ed;* Inflectional Ending *-ing;* Possessives (singular); Inflectional Endings *-ed, -ing* (drop finale *e*); Inflectional Endings *-ed, -ing* (double final consonant); CVCe syllables; Prefixes *re-, un-, dis-;* Suffixes *-ful, -less;* Compound Words; Contractions with *'s, 're, 'll, 've;* Open Syllables; Contractions with *not (isn't, aren't, wasn't, weren't, hasn't, haven't, can't);* Inflectional Endings and Plurals (change *y* to *i*); Comparative Inflectional endings *-er, -est* ; Irregular Plurals; Abbreviations; *r*-Controlled Syllables; Plural Possessives; Prefixes *pre-, non-, mis-;* Consonant +*le* Syllables (+*le*, +*al*, +*el*)